IN THE DESERT

David M. Schwartz *is an award-winning author of children's books, on a wide variety of topics, loved by children around the world.* Dwight Kuhn's *scientific expertise and artful eye work together with the camera to capture the awesome wonder of the natural world.*

For a free color catalog describing Gareth Stevens Publishing's list of high-quality books and multimedia programs, call 1-800-542-2595 (USA) or 1-800-461-9120 (Canada). Gareth Stevens Publishing's Fax: (414) 225-0377. See our catalog, too, on the World Wide Web: gsinc.com.

Library of Congress Cataloging-in-Publication Data

Schwartz, David M.
  In the desert / by David M. Schwartz; photographs by Dwight Kuhn.
    p. cm. — (Look once, look again)
  Includes bibliographical references (p. 23) and index.
  Summary: Introduces, in simple text and photographs, the characteristics of
various animals that live in the desert. Includes a coyote, gecko, rattlesnake,
mouse, scorpion, and tarantula.
  ISBN 0-8368-2220-X (lib. bdg.)
  1. Desert animals—Juvenile literature. [1. Desert animals.] I. Kuhn, Dwight, ill.
II. Title. III. Series: Schwartz, David M. Look once, look again.
QL116.S34   1998
~~201.754~~ —dc21   98-15408
    574;9

This North American edition first published in 1998 by
Gareth Stevens Publishing
1555 North RiverCenter Drive, Suite 201
Milwaukee, Wisconsin 53212 USA

First published in the United States in 1997 by Creative Teaching Press, Inc., P.O. Box 6017, Cypress, California, 90630-0017.

Printed in the United States of America

1 2 3 4 5 6 7 8 9 02 01 00 99 98

IN THE DESERT

by David M. Schwartz

photographs by Dwight Kuhn

A SPRINGBOARDS INTO

SCIENCE

SERIES

Gareth Stevens Publishing

MILWAUKEE

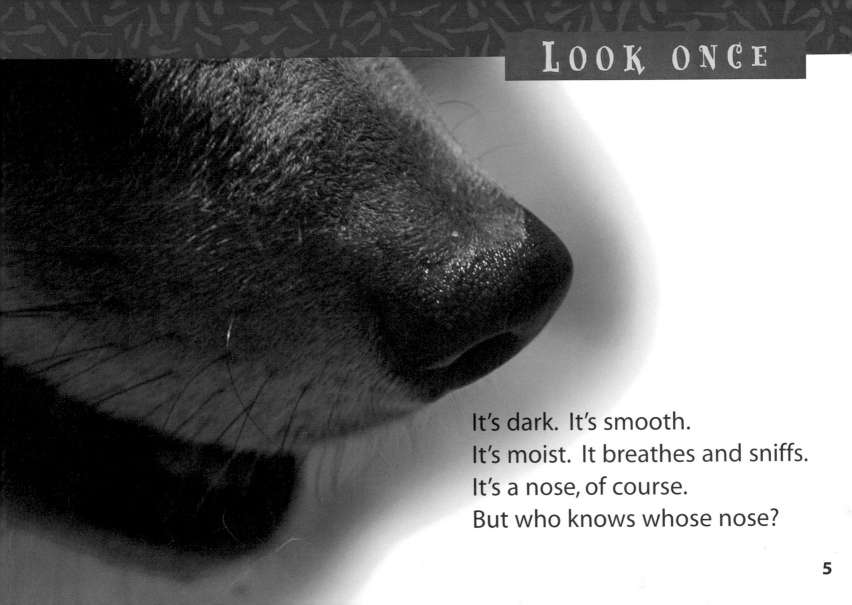

It's dark. It's smooth.
It's moist. It breathes and sniffs.
It's a nose, of course.
But who knows whose nose?

It's the nose of a coyote, and a very good nose it is! A coyote's nose is one million times better than your nose at smelling things. Thanks to its good sense of smell, a coyote can find food far away or under ground.

In bright light, this eye is just a narrow slit. After dark, it opens wide and looks for flies.

The eye belongs to a banded gecko. Geckos are lizards.
They can walk on walls, ceilings, and even windows.
Geckos will go almost anywhere to catch a fly!

Are these white spiders? Or are they part of a plant that wants to be left alone?

These are the spines
of a desert cactus.
Many desert animals
would love to eat the cactus
because it stores water in its stem.
But animals do not want
a mouthful of spines!

When spring rains come,
the cactus blooms with
colorful blossoms.

10

If you shake this, it will rattle. But you don't want to shake this kind of rattle! It belongs to a . . .

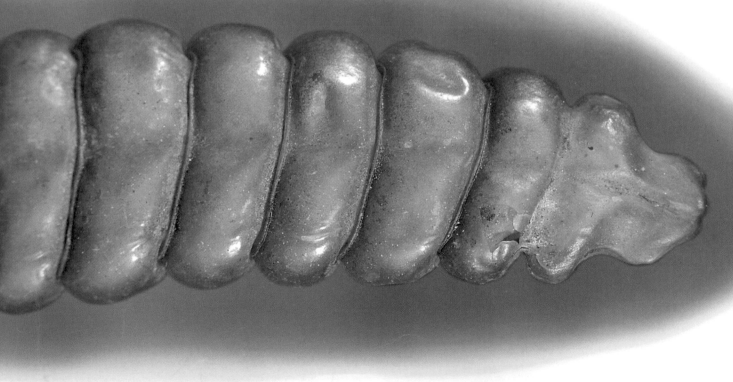

...rattlesnake! Poisonous snakes, like this diamondback rattlesnake, use their rattles to warn other animals to stay away.
They do not want to bite. They would rather be left in peace.

These long whiskers belong to a small animal with a keen sense of smell.

13

This mouse eats grasshoppers.
It is called a grasshopper mouse.
It uses its long whiskers
to sense when a coyote
is near. When it
feels movement, it
scurries off. It does
not want to be
a coyote's meal.

You might be stung by this if you get too close. Watch your step!

It's the stinger at the end of a scorpion's tail. A scorpion's stinger is filled with poison. If you sleep in the desert, shake out your shoes in the morning to make sure no scorpions have moved in!

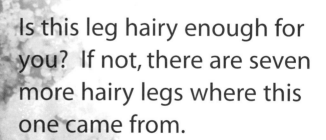

Is this leg hairy enough for you? If not, there are seven more hairy legs where this one came from.

Tarantulas are the world's biggest spiders. Some are so large they can eat lizards, small birds, and mice.

The hairs on a tarantula's legs vibrate slightly when other animals are moving nearby. The vibrations help the giant spider find its food.

A.

B.

C.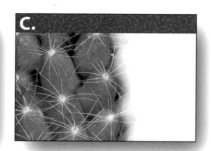

D.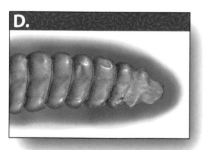

E.

F.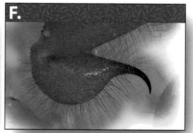

G.

Look closely. Can you name these plants and animals?

19

A.

Coyote

B.

Gecko

C.

Cactus

D.

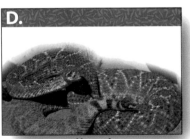

Diamondback
rattlesnake

E.

Grasshopper mouse

F.

Scorpion

G.

Tarantula

How many were you able to identify correctly?

banded gecko: a small lizard that lives in the desert. Geckos eat flies and other insects.

cactus: a type of plant that usually has spiny stems and grows in the desert.

coyote: an animal that is similar to a wolf, but smaller.

keen: very sharp or sensitive, such as keen eyesight.

lizard: a reptile with a long, scaly body. A gecko is a type of lizard.

poisonous: containing or having effects from toxins or poisons.

rattles: the dry rings at the end of a rattlesnake's tail that make a "rattle," or noisy sound.

scurries: moves with light running steps.

slit: a long, narrow opening.

sniff: to smell by taking short breaths in through the nose.

spines: parts of a plant that stick out and have sharp points.

stem: the main supporting part of a plant.

stinger: a sharp part on certain animals, such as scorpions, that can sting.

tarantula: a type of large, hairy spider.

vibrate: to move quickly back and forth.

whiskers: the long, stiff hairs that grow near the mouth of some animals.

Desert Garden-in-a-Bowl

Create a desert garden-in-a-bowl. Buy several small cacti. Place a layer of gravel on the bottom of a shallow bowl and cover it with a mix of two parts potting soil to one part sand. Have an adult help you plant the desert plants in the soil (after putting on gloves for protection from the spines). Find a spot for your garden in a sunny window and water it sparingly.

Alike and Different

Visit a botanical garden, conservatory, or garden center that features a collection of desert plants. How are the various kinds of plants that live in a desert similar? How are they different? What special qualities does each plant have to help it survive in a hot and dry habitat?

Where in the World?

Find a map that shows the deserts of the world. Which is the largest desert? Which is the smallest desert? Are there deserts in the United States and Canada? Is there an area where most of the world's deserts are concentrated? Where in the world can the desert plants and animals featured in this book be found?

Danger, Danger!

The rattlesnake uses the rattles on its tail to warn others to stay away. The skunk, meanwhile, warns animals and people by spraying a terrible-smelling scent. Can you think of any other animals that have their own particular ways of sending out a warning? Make a list of these animals and the warnings they use.

More Books to Read

Cactus Desert. Donald M. Silver (W. H. Freeman)
Coyotes. Sandra Lee (Child's World)
Exploring Deserts. Eco-Journey (series). Barbara J. Behm and Veronica Bonar (Gareth Stevens)
Fangs! (series). Eric Ethan (Gareth Stevens)
The New Creepy Crawly Collection (series). (Gareth Stevens)
Watching Desert Wildlife. Caroline Arnold (Lerner Group)

Videos

Animals of the Desert. (Phoenix/BFA Films)
The Cactus: Profile of a Plant. (Encyclopædia Britannica Educational Corporation)
Desert Animals and Plants.   (Wood Knapp Video)
Desert Creatures. (Encyclopædia Britannica Educational Corporation)

Web Sites

www.desertusa.com
/sunflower.singnet.com.sg/~liviafyk/cactus.html

Some web sites stay current longer than others. For further web sites, use your search engines to locate the following topics: *cacti, coyotes, deserts, lizards, rattlesnakes,* and *scorpions.*

INDEX